ACHIEVE 100

Grammar, Punctuation and Spelling

PRACTICE QUESTIONS

Marie Lallaway

RISING STARS

Acknowledgements

Rising Stars is grateful to the following schools who will be utilising Achieve to prepare their students for the National Tests: Chacewater Community Primary School, Cornwall; Coppice Primary School, Essex; Edgewood Primary School, Notts; Henwick Primary School, Eltham; Norwood Primary School, Southport; Sacred Heart Catholic Primary School, Manchester; Sunnyfields Primary School, Hendon; Tennyson Road Primary School, Luton.

Every effort has been made to trace all copyright holders, but if any have been inadvertently overlooked, the Publishers will be pleased to make the necessary arrangements at the first opportunity.

Although every effort has been made to ensure that website addresses are correct at time of going to press, Rising Stars cannot be held responsible for the content of any website mentioned in this book. It is sometimes possible to find a relocated web page by typing in the address of the home page for a website in the URL window of your browser.

Hachette UK's policy is to use papers that are natural, renewable and recyclable products and made from wood grown in sustainable forests. The logging and manufacturing processes are expected to conform to the environmental regulations of the country of origin.

ISBN: 978 1 78339 540 8

© Rising Stars UK Ltd 2015

First published in 2015 by Rising Stars UK Ltd, part of Hodder Education, an Hachette UK Company
Reprinted 2016 (twice), 2017 (three times), 2018

Carmelite House

50 Victoria Embankment

London EC4Y 0DZ

www.risingstars-uk.com

Author: Marie Lallaway

Series Editor: Maddy Barnes

Accessibility Reviewer: Vivien Kilburn

Educational Adviser: Josh Lury

Publishers: Kate Jamieson and Gillian Lindsey

Project Manager: Estelle Lloyd

Editorial: Dodi Beardshaw, Rachel Evans, Amanda George, Fiona Leonard

Cover design: Burville-Riley Partnership

Text design and typeset by the Pen and Ink Book Company Ltd

Printed by Ashford Colour Press Ltd.

A catalogue record for this title is available from the British Library.

Contents

The answers can be found in a pull-out section in the middle of this book.

Welcome to Achieve Key Stage 2 GPS Practice Questions 100

In this book you will find lots of practice and information to help you achieve the expected scaled score of 100 in the Key Stage 2 English Grammar, Punctuation and Spelling (GPS) tests.

About the Key Stage 2 Grammar, Punctuation and Spelling National Tests

The tests will take place in the summer term in Year 6. They will be done in your school and will be marked by examiners – not by your teacher.

The tests are didvided into two papers:

Paper 1: questions – 45 minutes (50 marks)

- You will answer short questions about grammar, punctuation and language strategies.
- Some questions will ask you to tick a box, circle or underline. Other questions will ask you to add words to a sentence, or to rewrite it making a change. You may be asked to explain why a sentence is written in a particular way.
- The questions will include the language of grammar and punctuation.
- Most questions are worth 1 mark, but you should check to make sure before you answer each question in case you need to give more than one answer.

Paper 2: spelling – approximately 15 minutes (20 marks)

- Twenty questions will be read aloud to you, one at a time. You will be asked to spell a particular word in each sentence. Some words may require a correctly placed apostrophe.
- The words may be taken from the word lists for Years 1–6.
- Each correct answer is worth 1 mark.

Test techniques

Before the tests

- Try to revise little and often, rather than in long sessions.
- Choose a time of day when you are not tired or hungry.
- Choose somewhere quiet so you can focus.
- Revise with a friend. You can encourage and learn from each other.
- Read the 'Top tips' throughout this book to remind you of important points in answering test questions.

During the tests

- READ THE QUESTION AND READ IT AGAIN.
- If you find a question difficult to answer, move on; you can always come back to it later.
- Always answer a multiple-choice question. If you really can't work out the answer, have a guess.
- Check to see how many marks a question is worth. Have you written enough to 'earn' those marks in your answer?
- Read the question again after you have answered it. Make sure you have given the correct number of answers within a question, e.g. Tick **two** boxes.
- If you have any time left at the end, go back to the questions you have missed. If you really do not know the answers, make guesses.

Where to get help:

- **Pages 6–29** practise grammar.
- **Pages 30–35** practise punctuation.
- **Pages 36–49** practise spelling. (Note that in the test the words for you to spell will be read to you in a sentence. These pages cannot replicate that format, so instead they allow you to practise spelling lots of common words that might appear in the test.)
- The answers can be found in a pull-out section in the middle of this book.

Nouns

To achieve 100 you need to know what nouns are and how to use them.

1 Circle all the **nouns** in the passage below.

Our holiday was fantastic. We visited beaches, mountains and even walked around a volcano.

1

(1 mark)

2 Add one **noun** to the sentence below.

Adele understands _____.

2

(1 mark)

3 Rewrite the sentence below, changing the **noun** to create another sentence that makes sense. Remember to punctuate your answer correctly.

Your idea is super.

_____

3

(1 mark)

4 Identify the **adjectives**, **nouns** and **verbs** in the sentence below. Write **A** (**adjective**), **N** (**noun**) and **V** (**verb**) in the correct boxes.

Danny saw an enormous web when he climbed up to the dusty attic.

4

(1 mark)

5 Underline the **nouns** in the sentence below.

Archie has a wonderful imagination and he turns his thoughts into words when he writes.

5

(1 mark)

> **! Top tip**
> • Always check how many nouns you have been asked to identify.

/ 5

Total for this page

Adjectives

To achieve 100 you need to know what adjectives are and how to use them.

1 Read the sentence below. Which words are **adjectives**?

Unfortunately, our ancient car broke down and we had a very long wait for help to arrive.

Tick **one**.

unfortunately, very ☐

broke, had ☐

ancient, long ☐

down, to ☐

(1 mark) 1

2 Identify the **adjective**, **noun** and **verb** in the sentence below.

Write **A** (**adjective**), **N** (**noun**) and **V** (**verb**) in the correct boxes.

John and Anne collected some unusual shells on the beach today.
     ↑   ↑   ↑
     ☐   ☐   ☐

(1 mark) 2

3 Rewrite the sentence below, changing the **adjective** for another suitable one. Remember to punctuate your answer correctly.

You have a lovely smile.

_____ .

(1 mark) 3

4 Underline all the **adjectives** in the passage below.

It was a dark and dreary night. Only the sound of the whistling wind could be heard.

(1 mark) 4

5 Tick one box in each row to show whether the underlined word is used as an **adjective** or an **adverb**.

Sentence	Adjective	Adverb
This is my <u>last</u> day at school.		
Joe ran his best but came <u>last</u> in the race.		
According to my grandmother, I am growing <u>taller</u> every week.		
There is a very <u>tall</u> tree in front of my house.		

(1 mark) 5

/ 5

Total for this page

7

Verbs

To achieve 100 you need to know what verbs are and how to use them.

1 Tick one box to show the **verb** in the sentence below.

Jo, the oldest girl in my class, often wears a funny hat.

☐ 1 *(1 mark)*

2 Circle the correct **verb form** to complete the sentence below.

Yesterday, I **push / pushed** my little brother on the swings when we **go / went** to the park.

☐ 2 *(1 mark)*

3 Complete the sentence with the correct **verb forms**.

Hardeep always _____ with Jess after school unless he

_____ to football practice.

☐ 3 *(1 mark)*

4 Underline all the **verbs** in the passage below.

I love vegetables but my sister prefers sweet things. Her teeth are quite bad.

☐ 4 *(1 mark)*

5 Tick the sentences that contain a **verb** in the past tense.

Sentence	Tick
He spilled his drink on the carpet.	
Please pass the bread.	
Someone knocked on the door.	
I think about you often.	

☐ 5 *(1 mark)*

/ 5

Total for this page

Adverbs

To achieve 100 you need to know what adverbs are, how to form them and how to use them.

1 Underline the **adverb** in the sentence below.

Robert was totally confused by the instructions.

	1

(1 mark)

2 Circle all the **adverbs** in the sentence below.

The very playful puppy wagged its tail furiously while watching the ball carefully for any sign of movement.

	2

(1 mark)

3 Rewrite the sentence below, adding a suitable **adverb**. Remember to punctuate your answer correctly.

James answered the last question.

	3

(1 mark)

4 Tick the sentences that contain an **adverb**.

My cup is empty. ☐

I will meet you later. ☐

She waited by the door. ☐

Can you see me now? ☐

	4

(1 mark)

5 Rewrite the sentence below adding an **adverb**. Remember to punctuate your answer correctly.

The door opened.

	5

(1 mark)

! Top tip

• Most 'how' adverbs end in *-ly* but not all of them. Look out for other ones such as work *hard*, run *fast*, drive *straight*.

/5

Total for this page

9

Modal verbs

To achieve 100 you need to know what modal verbs are and how to use them.

1 Tick two boxes to show the **modal verbs** in the sentence below.

I might be able to come swimming with you if you can collect me from

my house.

(1 mark) 1

2 Which of the events in the sentences below is the **most likely** to happen?

We could go to the cinema today. ☐

He can come to my house tomorrow. ☐

She will buy some new books today. ☐

They might have pizza for tea today. ☐

(1 mark) 2

3 Which of the events in the sentences below is the **least likely** to happen?

They might go to the coast tomorrow. ☐

I will help you. ☐

We can go fishing this afternoon. ☐

(1 mark) 3

4 Rewrite the sentence below to include a **modal verb** that expresses certainty. Remember to punctuate your answer correctly.

We swim every day.

(1 mark) 4

5 Underline the **modal verb** in the passage below.

Alex watched the plane approaching. He hoped that it might be bringing his father home.

(1 mark) 5

/ 5

Total for this page

Adverbials

To achieve 100 you need to identify and construct an adverbial.

1 Underline the **adverbials** in the sentences below.

I have hidden some treasure at the end of the garden.

In a few minutes they will arrive.

1

(1 mark)

2 Rewrite the sentence below so that it begins with the **adverbial**. Remember to punctuate your answer correctly.

We tidied up before we left.

_____

2

(1 mark)

3 Add an **adverbial** to the sentence below.

She will meet you _____.

3

(1 mark)

4 Tick the sentences that contain an **adverbial**.

Sentence	Tick
Dionne collected shells from the beach.	
Angela played by the edge of the sea.	
Kim ate her delicious sandwiches.	
Josh tried to arrive on time.	

4

(1 mark)

5 Tick the boxes to show which parts of the sentence are **adverbials**.

The children watched with great attention as the show began.

5

(1 mark)

/5

Total for this page

11

Pronouns

To achieve 100 you need to know what pronouns are and how to use them.

1 Tick the **pronouns** used in the sentence below.

1 ☐ *(1 mark)*

Oscar was meeting his uncle from the airport but the car broke down so he was late.

airport	car	☐
his	he	☐
Oscar	uncle	☐
but	so	☐

2 Circle the **pronouns** in the passage below.

2 ☐ *(1 mark)*

Beth was late for school. She never could get out of her bed in time. It was far too comfortable.

3 Rewrite the sentence below using a **pronoun**. Remember to punctuate your answer correctly.

3 ☐ *(1 mark)*

Olivia dances very well.

4 Underline one **pronoun** in each of the sentences below.

4 ☐ *(1 mark)*

That picture is mine.

The kitten has lost its ball.

What will you do next?

Please give the book to me.

5 Circle the **pronouns** in the sentence below.

5 ☐ *(1 mark)*

While he was paddling in the sea, Samir found a huge shell for his collection.

! Top tip
- You can decide if a word is a pronoun by testing whether you can replace it with a noun.

/ 5

Total for this page

Prepositions

To achieve 100 you need to identify prepositions and be able to use them.

1 Circle two **prepositions** in the sentence below.

The tortoise is in the garden under the bushes.

2 Add a suitable **preposition** to the sentence below.

Because we are near an airport, planes regularly fly _____ our school.

3 Rewrite the sentence below, changing the **preposition**. Remember to punctuate your answer correctly.

You coat is hanging beside mine.

_____

4 Circle all the **prepositions** in the passage below.

Hazel went to Scotland by train and had lunch in the restaurant carriage.

5 Tick one box in each row to show whether the word <u>after</u> is used as a **conjunction** or as a **preposition**.

Sentence	Conjunction	Preposition
We arrived <u>after</u> breakfast.		
The bus left <u>after</u> everyone got on.		
It will be sunny <u>after</u> the rain.		

Determiners

To achieve 100 you need to know what determiners are and how to use them.

1 Add the correct **determiners**, <u>a</u> or <u>an</u>, to each gap in the sentence below.

I am going to buy _____ yellow shirt, _____ orange scarf and _____ purple jumper.

☐ 1
(1 mark)

2 Underline all the **determiners** in the sentence below.

Alex needs more paints to finish her picture but we don't have any left.

☐ 2
(1 mark)

3 Rewrite the sentence, changing the **determiner**. Remember to punctuate your answer correctly.

Can I borrow the calculator?

_____

☐ 3
(1 mark)

4 Circle all the **determiners** in the sentence below.

Susie doesn't like this book but she would like to borrow that magazine.

☐ 4
(1 mark)

5 Add a suitable **determiner** to the sentence below.

The birds don't like these seeds but they do like _____ pieces of bread over there.

☐ 5
(1 mark)

! Top tip

- Remember that *an* is used in front of a word beginning with a vowel: *a e i o u* or a silent *h* (an hour).

☐ / 5
Total for this page

Statements, exclamations, commands and questions

To achieve 100 you need to recognise and use statement, exclamation, command and question sentences.

1 Add a **question mark** or an **exclamation mark** to the sentences below.

How delightful you are___

How did you do that___

What an appalling mess___

What species of insect is that___

□ 1
(1 mark)

2 Write a **statement** to answer this **question**. Remember to punctuate your answer correctly.

What are you doing at the weekend?

_____

□ 2
(1 mark)

3 Change this **command** to a **question**. Remember to punctuate your answer correctly.

Tell me your age.

_____

□ 3
(1 mark)

4 Are the sentences below **statements** or **commands**?

Sentence	Statement	Command
You all need to understand so listen carefully to the instructions.		
My tyre was punctured straightaway by some broken glass.		
Before you leave, pick up the rubbish.		
We must make a bonfire to burn all these fallen leaves.		

□ 4
(1 mark)

/ 4
Total for this page

! Top tip

- Read the sentences in an expressive voice – like a character in a story. Do this in your head.

15

Conjunctions

To achieve 100 you need to know the different conjunctions and be able to use them.

1 Use the **conjunctions** in the box to complete the sentence below. Use each conjunction only once.

| but   or   and |

You can have toast _____ butter _____ cereals for your breakfast _____ you can't have cake.

2 Write a **subordinating conjunction** to complete the sentence below.

Katie and Nisha spent a lot of time together _____ they went on their summer holiday.

3 Underline two **conjunctions** in the sentence below.

Ali can sing while he plays the guitar unless his friends make him laugh.

4 Add the correct **conjunction** from the box to the sentence below.

| if   when   since   despite |

Max has lived in the same house _____ he was born.

5 Tick the boxes to show the **coordinating conjunctions** in the passage below.

Everyone was excited because they were waiting for the magician who ☐ ☐

could breathe fire and make birds appear from her cloak. I was a little ☐

nervous but I still wanted to see. ☐

> **! Top tips**
> - A conjunction is usually found near the middle of a sentence, or at the beginning.
> - Look out for the two parts of a sentence and find the word that joins them together.

Main clauses and subordinate clauses

To achieve 100 you need to recognise and use main and subordinate clauses.

1 Tick the box to show the **subordinate clause** in each of the sentences below.

The birds all scattered | when the cat came into the garden.

☐ ☐

As soon as the bread was finished, | the ducks all swam away.

☐ ☐

1 (1 mark)

2 Which option correctly introduces the **subordinate clause** in the sentence below?

Abigail wanted to go to the cinema _____ she was very tired.

even though ☐
furthermore ☐
despite ☐
unless ☐

2 (1 mark)

3 Underline the **subordinate clause** in the sentence below.

It would be lovely to see you if you can come to the party.

3 (1 mark)

4 Add the correct words from the box to complete the **subordinate clauses** in the sentences below. Use each word only once.

| if   although   before |

a) Joe was trying to finish his computer game _____ he was called for his supper.

4a (1 mark)

b) I enjoy football practice _____ I do get very cold in the winter.

4b (1 mark)

c) Maisie thought she could win the race _____ she tried hard enough.

4c (1 mark)

/ 6

Total for this page

17

!Top tip

- Does the clause make sense on its own? If so, it is a main clause. If not, it is a subordinate clause.

Relative clauses

To achieve 100 you need to recognise and use relative clauses.

1 Tick one box to show which part of the sentence is a **relative clause**.

My grandfather has lived in the village where he was born for 80 years.

☐ ☐ ☐ ☐

☐ 1

(1 mark)

2 Circle the **relative clause** in the sentence below.

The snakes that can be found in England are usually harmless.

☐ 2

(1 mark)

3 Which of the sentences below contain a **relative clause**?

Tick **two**.

My pet rat, who is called Ronnie, is very intelligent. ☐

Archie's homework was left on the table by the door. ☐

Football practice which is usually on Mondays will be on Friday this week. ☐

Keela likes to read before bedtime. ☐

☐ 3

(1 mark)

4 Underline the **relative clause** in the sentence below.

The sunshine that is coming through the window today is beautiful.

(1 mark)

5 Rewrite the sentence below adding a **relative clause**. Remember to punctuate your answer correctly.

Max lives in Wales.

(1 mark)

_____

! **Top tip**

• Don't forget '*that*' is a relative pronoun as well as *who, which, where* and *when*.

/ 5

Total for this page

Subordinating and coordinating conjunctions

To achieve 100 you need to recognise and use subordinating and coordinating conjunctions.

1 Add **conjunctions** from the box to complete the sentences below. Use each conjunction only once.

| or   so   but |

a) The museum is shut _____ we can't visit today.

b) We could go to the park _____ the river.

c) I'd love to come to your party _____ I am going on holiday that day.

1a
(1 mark)

1b
(1 mark)

1c
(1 mark)

2 Circle all the **conjunctions** in the passage below.

Oscar has begun collecting unusual stones although he doesn't have many at present because he is waiting to go for a walk in the forest with his family.

2
(1 mark)

3 Add a suitable **conjunction** to the sentence below.

Basketball practice will begin _____ everyone has changed into their kits.

3
(1 mark)

4 Which option correctly introduces the **subordinate clause** in the sentence below?

We won't be going to the beach today _____ the weather changes and the sun comes out.

Tick **one**.

despite ☐

in spite of ☐

otherwise ☐

unless ☐

4
(1 mark)

/ 6

Total for this page

19

Noun phrases

To achieve 100 you need to recognise and use noun phrases.

1 Underline the longest possible **noun phrase** in the sentence below.

Hester found a tiny baby bird.

2 Add two suitable words to the **noun phrase** in the sentence below.

David had made a _____ _____ model castle.

3 Rewrite the sentence below, adding to the **noun phrase**. Remember to punctuate your answer correctly.

I have a new bicycle.

_____.

4 Underline the longest possible **noun phrase** in the sentence below.

The tree at the end of the road is going to be cut down.

5 Circle all the **noun phrases** in the sentence below.

For my next birthday, I would like a new pair of trainers.

6 Tick the sentences that contain a **noun phrase**.

Let's go fishing. ☐

Have you seen my new computer game? ☐

Please pass me the packet of biscuits. ☐

Josh can run very fast. ☐

Subject and object

To achieve 100 you need to find the subject and object in sentences.

1 Which of the sentences below contain an **object**?

Tick **two**.

I can sing loudly but not tunefully. ☐

Pass me the pepper please. ☐

We will watch a film this evening. ☐

This cake you made is delicious. ☐

1 ☐ *(1 mark)*

2 Tick the boxes to show the **subjects** in the passage below.

Anna needed to go the shop. She wanted to buy some eggs to make
☐   ☐ ☐   ☐

a cake.
☐

2 ☐ *(1 mark)*

3 Write **S** (**subject**) and **O** (**object**) in each box.

The class is organising a secret party for their teacher. She is moving to
☐   ☐   ☐

Australia to live.
☐

3 ☐ *(1 mark)*

4 Rewrite the sentence below changing the **subject**. Remember to punctuate your answer correctly.

Sam enjoys playing tennis.

_____

4 ☐ *(1 mark)*

5 Rewrite the sentence below changing the **object**. Remember to punctuate your answer correctly.

Ellie painted a picture.

_____

5 ☐ *(1 mark)*

☐ / 5

Total for this page

21

Subject and verb agreement

To achieve 100 you need to make the subject and verb in a sentence agree.

1 Circle the correct **subject** to match the **verb** in this sentence.

They / He like to watch a film on Friday evenings.

2 Write the correct form of the **verb** in the gap.

go / goes

We always _____ to the mountains for our holiday as

enjoy / enjoys

everyone in my family _____ walking.

3 Circle the correct **verb** to complete the sentence below.

The flock of sheep **is / are** being chased by a dog.

4 Are the **subject** and **verb** correct in the sentences below?
Tick one box in each row.

Sentence	Correct	Incorrect
The traffic jam are getting worse.		
The chicks are hatching from their eggs.		
Pollution is becoming a big problem in some cities.		
A herd of cows are grazing in the field.		

5 Rewrite the sentence below to make the **verb** agree with the **subject**. Remember to punctuate your answer correctly.

The circus are coming to our town.

_____

> ⭐ **Top tip**
> - Look out for nouns that refer to a set of things (e.g. a class, a collection, a government). They contain more than one thing, but act as one set, so are singular.

Verbs in the simple present and simple past tenses

To achieve 100 you need to recognise the simple present and simple past tenses and be able to construct these verb forms.

1 Circle all the verbs in the **simple past** tense in the sentence below.

☐ 1
(1 mark)

At the end of the weekend, everyone went home and slept well after a busy holiday.

2 Rewrite the sentence below in the **simple present** tense. Remember to punctuate your answer correctly.

☐ 2
(1 mark)

The river was frozen.

_____

3 Tick the correct verb form to complete the sentence below in the **simple past** tense.

☐ 3
(1 mark)

During the performance, the audience _____ as the tight-rope walker wobbled dangerously.

Tick **one**.

gasp ☐

will gasp ☐

gasped ☐

have gasped ☐

4 Write the verbs in the gaps in the **simple present** form.

☐ 4
(1 mark)

| to come |
↓

Each year, a little bird _____ to nest in my garden and

| to fly |
↓

_____ away at the end of the summer.

/4

Total for this page

23

Verbs in the progressive and perfect tenses

To achieve 100 you need to recognise the present and past progressive tenses and the present and past perfect tenses and be able to construct these verb forms.

1 Tick one box to show the **past progressive** verb form to complete the sentence below.

While he _____ on the swings, I went up and down the slide.

Tick **one**.

plays ☐

playing ☐

was playing ☐

is playing ☐

2 Write the verb in the gap in the **past progressive** form.

to roar

The lions _____ loudly in the distance.

3 Underline the verb that is in the **present progressive** tense in the sentence below.

We will stay in because it is pouring outside.

4 Which sentence is written using the **present perfect** tense?

Tick **one**.

Sheena has owned her pony for two years. ☐

Alex wants to learn to ride. ☐

Aidan used to have two pet goats. ☐

Rita is going to get a pet pig. ☐

☐ 1
(1 mark)

☐ 2
(1 mark)

☐ 3
(1 mark)

☐ 4
(1 mark)

/ 4

Total for this page

24

5 In the sentence below, Thomas watched the film on his own before he watched it with his friend.

Add a suitable **verb** to complete the sentence:

Although Thomas _____ seen the film before, he was happy to watch it again with his friend.

6 Tick a box in each row to show whether the sentence is written in the **present progressive** or the **past progressive** tense.

Sentence	Present progressive	Past progressive
The children were learning about Greek legends.		
This computer isn't working very well.		
We are choosing what we want to do today.		
She was carefully pouring the water from the jug.		

7 Add the correct verb form to the sentence below.

to have
↓

Before I even started my lunch, Ethan _____ finished his completely.

8 Rewrite the sentence below using the **past progressive** verb form. Remember to punctuate your answer correctly.

I am swimming.

_____

! Top tip
- Progressive tenses have two parts:
  Use the *i* in *progressive* to remind you of the *i* in *-ing*.

Passive and active voices

To achieve 100 you need to recognise the active and passive voices.

1   Tick one box to show the sentence below that is in the **passive voice**.

Tick **one**.

You need to be very gentle with hamsters. ☐

Cheetahs can run at incredible speeds. ☐

The new tropical fish was placed carefully in its tank. ☐

The elephants travelled a long way to the watering-hole. ☐

□ 1
(1 mark)

2   Tick one box in each row to show whether the sentence is in the **active** or **passive** voice.

Sentence	Active	Passive
The rocks have been eroded by the sea.		
The sea is eroding the rocks.		
Waves are crashing onto the beach.		
The beach was destroyed by the storm.		

□ 2
(1 mark)

3   Rewrite the sentence below in the **passive voice**. Remember to punctuate your answer correctly.

The astronomer discovered a new star.

□ 3
(1 mark)

4   Rewrite the sentence below in the **active voice**. Remember to punctuate your answer correctly.

Charlie was woken by the light from the window.

□ 4
(1 mark)

/4
Total for this page

Answers

All answers are worth 1 mark, unless otherwise indicated.

Nouns (page 6)

1 circle: holiday; beaches; mountains; volcano
2 Accept any suitable noun that makes sense with correct punctuation, e.g. Adele understands French/things.
3 Accept any suitable change that makes sense, e.g. Your bike/gift/suggestion is super.
The sentence must be correctly punctuated.
4 A = enormous/dusty;
N = web/attic; V = saw/climbed
5 underline: Archie; imagination; thoughts; words

Adjectives (page 7)

1 tick: ancient, long
2 A = unusual; N = beach;
V = collected
3 Accept any suitable change of adjective with correct punctuation, e.g. You have a beautiful/terrifying/huge smile.
The sentence must be correctly punctuated.
4 underline: dark; dreary; whistling
5 This is my last day at school.
adjective
Joe ran his best but came last in the race. adverb
According to my grandmother, I am growing taller every week. adverb
There is a very tall tree in front of my house. adjective

Verbs (page 8)

1 tick: wears
2 circle: pushed; went
3 plays; goes
4 underline: love; prefers; are
5 tick: He spilled his drink on the carpet.
Someone knocked on the door.

Adverbs (page 9)

1 underline: totally
2 circle: very; furiously; carefully
3 Accept any suitable adverb addition that makes sense with correct punctuation, e.g. James answered the very last question./

James quickly answered the last question./James answered the last question easily.
The sentence must be correctly punctuated.
4 tick: I will meet you later.
Can you see me now?
5 Accept the addition of a suitable adverb in a suitable position with correct punctuation, e.g. The door opened slowly./Suddenly, the door opened.
The sentence must be correctly punctuated.

Modal verbs (page 10)

1 tick: might; can
2 She will buy some new books today.
3 They might go to the coast tomorrow.
4 We will swim every day.
The sentence must be correctly punctuated.
5 underline: might

Adverbials (page 11)

1 underline: at the end of the garden; In a few minutes
2 Before we left, we tidied up.
The sentence must be correctly punctuated.
3 Accept any suitable adverbial addition that makes sense, e.g. She will meet you in a while/after dinner/by the duck pond.
4 tick: Dionne collected shells from the beach.
Angela played by the edge of the sea.
Josh tried to arrive on time.
5 tick: with great attention; as the show began

Pronouns (page 12)

1 tick: his he
2 circle: She; her; It
3 She dances very well.
The sentence must be correctly punctuated.
4 underline: mine; its; you; me
5 circle: he; his

Prepositions (page 13)

1 circle: in; under
2 Accept a suitable preposition

that makes sense with correct punctuation, e.g. over; above; around; near.
3 Accept a suitable preposition that makes sense, e.g. Your coat is hanging near/next to/over/below mine.
The sentence must be correctly punctuated.
4 circle: to; by; in
5 We arrived after breakfast.
preposition
The bus left after everyone got on.
conjunction
It will be sunny after the rain.
preposition

Determiners (page 14)

1 a; an; a
2 underline: more; any
3 Can I borrow a/that/this/one calculator?
The sentence must be correctly punctuated.
4 circle: this; that
5 those; the

Statements, exclamations, commands and questions (page 15)

1 How delightful you are!
How did you do that?
What an apalling mess!
What species of insect is that?
2 Accept any suitable statement that is a complete sentence with correct punctuation, e.g. *I am visiting my aunt* not *visiting my aunt.*
The sentence must be correctly punctuated.
3 Accept a suitable question that refers to age, e.g. What is your age?/How old are you?
The sentence must be correctly punctuated.
4 You all need to understand so listen carefully to the instructions. command
My tyre was punctured straightaway by some broken glass. statement
Before you leave, pick up the rubbish. command
We must make a bonfire to burn all these fallen leaves. statement

Conjunctions (page 16)
1 and; or; but
2 when
3 underline: while; unless
4 since
5 tick: and; but

Main clauses and subordinate clauses (page 17)
1 tick: when the cat…;
As soon as…
2 even though
3 underline: if you can come to the party.
4 a) before; b) although; c) if

Relative clauses (page 18)
1 tick: where he was born
2 circle: that can be found
3 tick: My pet rat, who is called Ronnie, is very intelligent.
Football practice which is usually on Mondays will be on Friday this week.
4 underline: that is coming through the window today
5 Accept a suitable relative clause that makes sense with correct punctuation, e.g. Max, who is five years old, lives in Wales.
The sentence must be correctly punctuated.

Subordinating and coordinating conjunctions (page 19)
1 a) so; b) or; c) but
2 circle: although; because
3 Accept a suitable conjunction that makes sense, e.g. as soon as; when; after.
4 unless

Noun phrases (page 20)
1 underline: a tiny baby bird
2 Accept any suitable adjectives, or an adverb with an adjective, e.g. brilliant, detailed; totally amazing; very large.
3 Accept any suitable additions to the noun phrase with correct punctuation, e.g. I have a brand/lovely/really great new bicycle or I have a new red bicycle with knobbly tyres.
The sentence must be correctly punctuated.
4 underline: The tree at the end of the road
5 circle: For my next birthday; a new pair of trainers

6 tick: Have you seen my new computer game?
Please pass me the packet of biscuits.

Subject and object (page 21)
1 tick: Pass me the pepper please.
We will watch a film this evening.
2 tick: Anna; She
3 class = S; party = O; She = S; Australia = O
4 Accept any suitable answer that changes the subject 'Sam' and continues to make sense with correct punctuation, e.g. Alice/He enjoys playing tennis.
The sentence must be correctly punctuated.
5 Accept any suitable answer that changes the object 'picture' with correct punctuation, e.g. her nails; the wall.
The sentence must be correctly punctuated.

Subject and verb agreement (page 22)
1 circle: They
2 go; enjoys
3 circle: is
4 The traffic jam are getting worse. incorrect
The chicks are hatching from their eggs. correct
Pollution is becoming a big problem in some cities. correct
A herd of cows are grazing in the field. incorrect
5 The circus is coming to our town.
The sentence must be correctly punctuated.

Verbs in the simple present and simple past tenses (page 23)
1 circle: went; slept
2 The river is frozen.
The sentence must be correctly punctuated.
3 tick: gasped
4 comes; flies

Verbs in the progressive and perfect tenses (pages 24–25)
1 tick: was playing
2 were roaring
3 underline: is pouring
4 tick: Sheena has owned her pony for two years.
5 had
6 The children were learning about

Greek legends. past
This computer isn't working very well. present
We are choosing what we want to do today. present
She was carefully pouring the water from the jug. past
7 had
8 I was swimming.
The sentence must be correctly punctuated.

Passive and active voices (pages 26–27)
1 tick: The new tropical fish was placed carefully in its tank.
2 The rocks have been eroded by the sea. passive
The sea is eroding the rocks. active
Waves are crashing onto the beach. active
The beach was destroyed by the storm. passive
3 Accept answers that include or do not include the agent with correct punctuation, e.g. A new star was discovered (by the astronomer).
The sentence must be correctly punctuated.
4 The light from the window woke Charlie.
The sentence must be correctly punctuated.
5 was moved
6 The pyramids were built many years ago. passive
Roman ruins have been found in our town. passive
The Romans invaded England. active
In Egypt you can see the river Nile. active
7 lives
8 A glass was knocked over by the cat when it jumped on the table.
The sentence must be correctly punctuated.

Subjunctive verb forms (page 28)
1 tick: were
2 underline: were
3 save
4 underline: were
5 [2 marks] Kim wished that she were home already.
The sentence must be correctly punctuated.

Standard English and formality (page 29)

1 circle: were; was
2 The sentence must be correctly punctuated.
  Those shoes are mine not yours.
3 'are required' is more formal
4 The sentence must be correctly punctuated.
  He isn't/is not coming.
5 circle: consider; assist; invited; exit

Capital letters, full stops, exclamation marks and question marks (page 30)

1 underline: wednesday; harvey
2 The chair broke and Sarah Robinson fell on the floor.
  The sentence must be correctly punctuated.
3 How are you feeling?
  How hard you've been working!
  However you arrange the tables is fine with me.
4 a) last week, we went to see our friend, marcus.
  b) Accept answers that refer to 'Last' requiring a capital letter because it begins a sentence, and 'Marcus' because it is a proper noun/name of a person.

Commas (page 31)

1 We like to paddle, splash, swim and play in the sea when we go on our holiday.
2 If Carlos can answer the next question, we will win the quiz.
  Miriam plays football, basketball and tennis each week.
  Lucy likes playing with her dogs, Caspar and Charlie.
3 With great determination, Henry took a breath and began to sing.
4 a) A comma is used to separate items in a list.
  b) A comma is used to separate clauses/divide two parts of the sentence.
5 Full of confidence, the team ran out onto the pitch.

Inverted commas (page 32)

1 tick: before 'When'; after 'visit?'
2 Answers should include correctly located punctuation.
  "I love a warm fire on a cold day," commented Gran.
  Callum replied, "I can light one for you now if you like."

3 Luke called, "Can I come too?"
4 Accept answers that refer to inverted commas showing what is spoken, e.g. they show what someone says.
5 Accept answers that use correct punctuation and transform the verb from past present tense, e.g. Elaine said, "I am happy to help."

Apostrophes (page 33)

1 tick: I can't dance very well.
  He's very fond of parrots.
2 hadn't/shouldn't
3 Sean's bag is blue and Ravinder's bag is red.
4 teams'

Parenthesis (page 34)

1 tick after: animals
2 It was very hot – baking, in fact – so I put on my suncream.
3 Gina, who had been practising hard, completed her gymnastics performance to much applause.
4 James talks all the time (he never stops) and drives us all mad.
5 My cat has had a litter of kittens – five in total – and they are all ginger.
6 The island is beautiful – stunning, actually – and there is a lot of wildlife.

Colons, semi-colons, single dashes, hyphens and bullet points (page 35)

1 tick after: ingredients
2 The light on the street corner flickered; it would soon be completely dark.
3 tick: The weather looks great; let's go for a picnic.
  I love a rainy day; it's a chance to splash in the puddles.
4 Greg won the competition – much to his surprise.
5 There are three gymnasts in my class: Millie, Max and Ayesha.

Prefixes and suffixes (page 36)

1 dis
2 unattractive; recount; preview
3 un
4 ful
5 underline: -ly; -ness; -er

Prefixes (page 37)

1 a) disappeared
  b) descent
  c) describe
  d) dissatisfied
2 a) delay
  b) disturb
  c) deliberate
  d) deny
3 descend   disagreement
  description   disabled
  dessert   disaster
  desperate   disbelieve
  deserve   disease
  destroy   disapproving
  desert   disgraceful

Suffixes: -tion, -ssion, -cian (pages 38–39)

1 a) tension
  b) expressions
  c) permission
  d) attention
  e) discussion
2 expand – expansion
  invent – invention
  complete – completion
  tense – tension
  collide – collision
  operate – operation
  react – reaction
  relate – relation
  decide – decison
  converse – conversion
3 a) station
  b) musician
  c) hesitation
  d) invention
  e) revision
4 attention, optician, decision, hesitation, version, consideration, politician, conversation, tension, mention

Suffixes: -ous, -tious, -cious (page 40)

1 a) axin + ous – anxious
  b) gernad + ous – dangerous
  c) iledic + ous – delicious
  d) malgor + ous – glamorous
  e) goerg + ous – gorgeous
  f) hilar + ous – hilarious
  g) vern + ous – nervous
2 a) various
  b) ambitious/anxious
  c) furious
  d) spacious
  e) curious
  f) glorious/hideous

g) poisonous

h) jealous

i) anxious

j) glorious

Suffixes: -able, -ably, -ible, -ibly (page 41)

1 a) comfortable

b) visible

c) understandably

d) reasonable

e) terribly

f) sensibly

g) possibly

h) dependable

i) identifiable

2 changeable; comfortable; extendable; convertible; reasonable; accessible

3 a) responsibly

b) divisible

c) collectable

d) indestructible

e) enjoyable

Suffixes: -ant, -ance, -ancy, -ent, -ence, -ency (page 42)

1 a) important

b) hesitant

c) independent

d) intelligent

e) assistant

f) silent

g) brilliant

h) confident

2 a) emergency

b) performance

c) distance

d) obedient

e) violence

f) sequence

3 a) impatient

b) tolerance

c) appearance

d) consequence

Words with ei, eigh, ey and ie/ei (page 43)

1 a) neighbours

b) eight

c) mischief

d) piece

e) weighs

2 a) ancient

b) neither

c) receive

d) prey

e) believe

3 sigleh – sleigh; grein – reign; tweigh – weight; cedivee – deceive; zeesi – seize; rieth – their; drifen – friend; ifecre – fierce

Words with ough (page 44)

1 a) rough

b) through

c) brought

d) ought

e) coughing

2 a) thought

b) thorough

c) fought

d) although

e) dough

3 touthgh – thought;
tunghoud – doughnut
onguth – nought
thruog – trough
ugoht – tough

Word endings: al, el, il, le (page 45)

1 a) medal

b) rumble

c) nostril

d) alphabetical

e) example

2 a) chemicals

b) swivel

c) cables

d) camels

e) traditional

3 marbels – marbles
gravle – gravel
beetel – beetle
jewles – jewels
possibel – possible
tropicel – tropical

Silent letters (page 46)

1 a) knuckle

b) ghosts

c) guards

d) autumn

e) island

f) wrist

g) knights

h) sign

i) thistles

j) answer

2 underline: wrong; knead; dough; exhausting; knew; would; knack

3 a) column

b) writing

c) honest

d) doubt

e) bomb

Homophones (page 47)

1 a) allowed

b) passed

c) heard

d) your

e) too

f) you're

g) brake

h) their

i) peace

j) guessed

2 Any suitable sentence that makes sense with correct punctuation, e.g. Mother gave a groan as the twins had grown out of their shoes again. When I got on the plane, it was plain to see that there wasn't a seat for me.
On the tropical isle, an aisle had been made between the trees for an aeroplane landing strip.
In the desert, it is difficult for an ice-cream dessert to survive.
This is our best hour.
We could sail to France and go to the sale of boats.
The battle was fought for the Roman fort.
The sentences must be correctly punctuated.

3 a) there

b) their

c) they're

Synonyms and antonyms (page 48)

1 tick: accident

2 tick: slow

3 tick: triumph

4 tick: timely

5 conscious   unaware
enough   insufficient
appear   vanish
deny   confirm

Word families (page 49)

1 tick: family; familiar

2 worth

3 Accept any suitable answer such as action; actor; actress; acting.

4 tick: attention; attendant; inattentive

5 Accept any suitable answers such as hardness; hardy; hardly; hard-working.

5 Complete the sentence in the **passive voice**.

to move

↓

The table _____ nearer to the window.

5

(1 mark)

6 Tick one box to show whether the sentence is written in the **active** or the **passive** voice.

Sentence	Active	Passive
The pyramids were built many years ago.		
Roman ruins have been found in our town.		
The Romans invaded England.		
In Egypt you can see the river Nile.		

6

(1 mark)

7 Complete the sentence below using the **active voice**.

to live

↓

Josh _____ by the sea.

7

(1 mark)

8 Rewrite the sentence below using the **passive voice**. Remember to punctuate your answer correctly.

The cat knocked over a glass when it jumped on the table.

_____

_____

8

(1 mark)

! Top tip

- Identify a passive sentence by checking who or what did the action. If the person (or thing) is not given in the sentence, it is passive. If the person (or thing) appears after the verb, it is a passive sentence.

/ 4

Total for this page

Subjunctive verb forms

To achieve 100 you need to recognise verbs in the subjunctive form.

1 Which option completes the sentence below so that it uses the **subjunctive** mood?

I wish I _____ able to help you with your homework, but I can't do it either.

Tick **one**.

could be ☐

were ☐

may be ☐

was ☐

1 (1 mark)

2 Underline the verb in the **subjunctive** form in the sentence below.

If I were you, I would save some sweets for later.

2 (1 mark)

3 Complete the sentence below using the **subjunctive** form. Choose one verb from the box.

| save | saves | will save | is saving |

I recommend that she _____ a little money each month.

3 (1 mark)

4 Underline the verb in the **subjunctive** mood in the sentence below.

Your teacher would be pleased if you were on time more regularly.

4 (1 mark)

5 Rewrite the sentence below so that it uses the **subjunctive** mood. Remember to punctuate your answer correctly.

Kim wished that she was home already.

5 (2 marks)

_____

! Top tip

• The subjunctive form often uses a verb in a way that doesn't feel quite usual. Look out for this.

/6

Total for this page

Standard English and formality

To achieve 100 you need to know how to identify and use Standard English, and to recognise differences between informal and formal language.

1 Circle one verb in each underlined pair to complete the sentences using **Standard English**.

They **was / were** hoping to visit their grandparents at the weekend.

He **was / were** first to arrive at school.

2 Rewrite the sentence below using **Standard English**. Remember to punctuate your answer correctly.

Them shoes are mine not yours.

3 Explain the effect of changing the words underlined in the sentences below.

You **have to** follow the instructions given by the tour guide.

You **are required** to follow the instructions given by the tour guide.

4 Rewrite the sentence below using **Standard English**. Remember to correctly punctuate your answer.

He ain't coming.

5 Circle the most **formal** vocabulary choice for the underlined words in each sentence.

You should **consider / think about** your answers more carefully.

Would you like me to **assist / help** you with those heavy bags?

Henry has **asked / invited** me to his party.

Please **exit / leave** the stadium by the west door.

Capital letters, full stops, exclamation marks and question marks

To achieve 100 you need to use capital letters, full stops, exclamation marks and question marks in the correct places in sentences.

1 Underline the words that should have **capital letters** in the sentence below.

On wednesday, we are taking our dog, harvey, to the vet.

	1

(1 mark)

2 Rewrite the passage below, correctly using **capital letters** and **full stops**.

the chair broke and sarah robinson fell on the floor

_____

	2

(1 mark)

3 Use the **punctuation** from the box to complete the sentences below. Use each form of punctuation only once.

! ? .

How are you feeling___

How hard you've been working___

However you arrange the tables is fine with me___

	3

(1 mark)

4 a) Circle the two letters that should be **capitals** in the sentence below.

last week, we went to see our friend, marcus.

	4a

(1 mark)

b) Explain why each of these letters should be a **capital**.

_____

_____

	4b

(1 mark)

Top tip

- Remember that all parts of proper nouns (e.g. *Sally Smith*, *United Kingdom*, *Rising Stars Publications*) need capital letters.

/5

Total for this page

30

Commas

To achieve 100 you need to use commas to mark clauses or phrases.

1 Correctly add **commas** to the sentence below.

We like to paddle splash swim and play in the sea when we go on our holiday.

_____

	1
(1 mark)	

2 Which of the sentences below correctly use **commas**?

If Carlos can answer the next question, we will win the quiz. ☐

Miriam plays football, basketball and tennis each week. ☐

Lucy likes playing with her dogs, Caspar and Charlie. ☐

Asa's aunt, who lives in Ireland is coming to visit. ☐

	2
(1 mark)	

3 Add a **comma** to the sentence below.

With great determination Henry took a breath and began to sing.

_____

	3
(1 mark)	

4 Explain why **commas** are used in the sentences below.

a) **I have learned to dance, sing and act on stage.**

_____

	4a
(1 mark)	

b) **When I first started to perform, I used to get very nervous.**

_____

	4b
(1 mark)	

5 Add a **comma** to the sentence below.

Full of confidence the team ran out onto the pitch.

_____

	5
(1 mark)	

> **! Top tip**
> • There should be no comma before the last item in a list.

/6
Total for this page

Inverted commas

To achieve 100 you need to use inverted commas to show speech.

1 Tick the boxes to show where the **inverted commas** should go in the sentence below.

When are you coming to visit? asked Andre.

2 Add **inverted commas**, one **comma** and one **full stop** to each of the sentences below.

I love a warm fire on a cold day commented Gran

Callum replied I can light one for you now if you like

3 Rewrite the sentence below using correct **punctuation** and capital letters.

Luke called can I come too

_____

4 Why are **inverted commas** used in the sentence below?

"How many pets do you have?" asked Danny.

_____

5 Rewrite the sentence below using **direct speech**.

Elaine said that she was happy to help.

_____

Apostrophes

To achieve 100 you need to use apostrophes correctly.

1 Tick the sentences that use **apostrophes** correctly.

I can't dance very well. ☐

He's very fond of parrots. ☐

Her notebook is full of doodle's. ☐

Our school does'nt allow dogs on the field. ☐

	1
	(1 mark)

2 Rewrite the underlined words in the sentence below, correctly using **apostrophes** to show contraction.

Jack <u>had not</u> finished clearing up his paints so he <u>should not</u> have put

_____   _____

his apron away.

	2
	(1 mark)

3 Rewrite the sentence below, correctly using **apostrophes**.

Seans bag is blue and Ravinders bag is red.

_____

	3
	(1 mark)

4 Rewrite the underlined word, correctly using an **apostrophe**.

All of the <u>teams</u> captains led their players out onto the sports field.

_____

	4
	(1 mark)

! Top tips

- *Its* and *It's* can be confusing. *It's* is only ever used to shorten *It is*.
- *Its* is used for possession. There is never an apostrophe used in *Its* for possession because it is a pronoun, like *his* or *her*.
- Nouns that refer to a group need a final *s* to show possession. Then, place the apostrophe before that *s*, e.g. *children's*, *herd's*, *people's*.

/ 4

Parenthesis

To achieve 100 you need to recognise the correct use of a parenthesis.

1 Tick two boxes to show where a pair of **brackets** should go.

My favourite animals snakes are not popular with everyone.

☐ ☐ ☐ ☐

(1 mark) 1

2 Which of these sentences uses **dashes** correctly?

It was very hot baking, in fact – so I put on – my suncream. ☐

It was – very hot – baking, in fact so I put on my suncream. ☐

It was very hot – baking, in fact – so I put on my suncream. ☐

It was very hot baking – in fact – so I put on my suncream. ☐

(1 mark) 2

3 Insert a pair of commas to show **parenthesis** in the sentence below.

Gina who had been practising hard completed her gymnastics performance to much applause.

(1 mark) 3

4 Add a pair of **brackets** to the sentence below.

James talks all the time he never stops and drives us all mad.

(1 mark) 4

5 Insert a pair of **dashes** in the sentence below.

My cat has had a litter of kittens five in total and they are all ginger.

(1 mark) 5

6 Rewrite the sentence below using **dashes** for parenthesis.

The island is beautiful stunning, actually and there is a lot of wildlife.

_____

_____

(1 mark) 6

/ 6

Total for this page

Colons, semi-colons, single dashes, hyphens and bullet points

To achieve 100 you need to identify and use punctuation correctly.

1 Tick the box to show where a **colon** should go in the sentence below.

My cake needs these ingredients flour, eggs, sugar and jam.

☐ ☐ ☐ ☐

(1 mark) 1

2 Add a **semi-colon** to the passage below.

The light on the street corner flickered it would soon be completely dark.

(1 mark) 2

3 Tick the sentences below that correctly use a **semi-colon**.

The weather looks great; let's go for a picnic. ☐

It is cold today so; shall we stay indoors by the fire. ☐

At the end of the day; I love to curl up with a good book. ☐

I love a rainy day; it's a chance to splash in the puddles. ☐

(1 mark) 3

4 Which of the sentences below correctly uses a **dash**?

Tick **one**.

Greg won – the competition much to his surprise. ☐

Greg won the competition – much to his surprise. ☐

Greg won the competition much – to his surprise. ☐

Greg won the competition much to – his surprise. ☐

(1 mark) 4

5 Insert a **colon** in the sentence below.

There are three gymnasts in my class Millie, Max and Ayesha.

(1 mark) 5

/ 5

Total for this page

35

Prefixes and suffixes

To achieve 100 you need to know how to add prefixes and suffixes to words.

1 Which **prefix** can be added to both of the words below?

_____appear

_____appoint

Prefix: _____

☐ 1

(1 mark)

2 Add a **prefix** from the box to each of the words below to make a new word.

Use each prefix only **once**.

pre / un / re

_____attractive _____count _____view

☐ 2

(1 mark)

3 Which **prefix** can be added to both of the words below?

appealing   helpful

_____

☐ 3

(1 mark)

4 Add a **suffix** to make this word an adjective.

truth_____

☐ 4

(1 mark)

5 Underline the **suffixes** in the words below.

rapidly   slowness   faster

☐ 5

(1 mark)

! Top tip
• Remember to keep the double letter if the prefix ends and the word begins with the same letter, e.g. *unnecessary*.

/ 5

Total for this page

Prefixes

To achieve 100 you need to correctly spell words with prefixes.

1 Circle the correct **spelling** of the word in each sentence.

a) The last slice of cake has **disappeared/disapeared**.

b) After climbing up the mountain, the **descent/discent** should be easier.

c) Can you **describe/desscribe** the burglar?

d) I am **disatisified/dissatisfied** with your work today.

1 (1 mark)

2 Choose the correct word from the box to complete each sentence.

deliberate delay disturb deny

a) There will be a long _____ at the airport.

b) Don't _____ your uncle when he is sleeping.

c) You are making a _____ effort to improve your spelling.

d) You cannot _____ that you were involved.

2 (1 mark)

3 Organise the words into two groups according to whether they begin with <u>des</u> or <u>dis</u>.

disagreement   descend   disabled   disaster   description
disbelieve   disease   dessert   disapproving   desperate
deserve   disgraceful   destroy   desert

des	dis

3 (2 marks)

Suffixes: *-tion, -ssion, -cian*

To achieve 100 you need to correctly spell words with these suffixes.

1   Circle the correct **spelling** in each sentence.

a)   The story builds to a moment of **tention / tension**.

b)   My grandfather has some unusual **expressions / expresions**.

c)   Can I have **permision / permission** to leave?

d)   You will need to pay **attenshun / attention** to the film.

e)   We need to have a **discussion / discucian** about your behaviour.

1
(1 mark)

2   Which of the verbs below can add the **suffix** -<u>sion</u> and which will use -<u>tion</u>?

Write the correct spelling of each noun.

expand   _____

invent   _____

complete   _____

tense   _____

collide   _____

operate   _____

react   _____

relate   _____

decide   _____

converse   _____

2
(2 marks)

/3

Total for this page

3 Write the correct word in each gap.

| revision   station   invention   musician   hesitation |

3

(1 mark)

a) I will meet you at the _____ .

b) I would like to be a _____ when I grow up.

c) Without a moment's _____ , he opened the door.

d) Computers are an important _____ .

e) Have you done enough _____ for your test?

4 Match the **beginnings** of the words below with the correct **ending**.

4

(2 marks)

atten

opti

deci

hesita

ver

considera

politi

conversa

ten

men

cian

tion

sion

! Top tip

- Remember: Ian has lots of jobs. So use *-ian* if the word is a job.

Suffixes: *-ous, -tious, -cious*

To achieve 100 you need to correctly spell words with these suffixes.

1 Each of these groups of letters contains the **suffix** -<u>ous</u>. Arrange the letters to find the words.

1

(1 mark)

a) axin + ous   a_____

b) gernad + ous   d_____

c) iledic + ous   d_____

d) malgor + ous   g_____

e) goerg + ous   g_____

f) ihilar + ous   h_____

g) vern + ous   n_____

2 Add the correct word from the box to the gap in each sentence. Some words fit more than one answer.

2

(2 marks)

ambitious	anxious	glorious	furious	various
poisonous	curious	hideous	jealous	spacious

a) There are_____ solutions to the problem.

b) Harry is _____about his future.

c) Your teacher will be_____ if you do that.

d) This is a _____ room.

e) I am _____ to find out more about dinosaurs.

f) What a _____ picture.

g) These plants can be_____.

h) My brother is _____of my new bike.

i) Jack is a little _____ about the race.

j) The party was a _____ success.

/3

40

Total for this page

Suffixes: *-able, -ably, -ible, -ibly*

To achieve 100 you need to correctly spell words with these suffixes.

1 Circle the correct **spelling** in each sentence.

a) That chair looks very **comfortible / comfortable**.

b) Your happiness is **visible / visable** on your face.

c) Andrew is **understandibly / understandably** upset by your remark.

d) That sounds like a **reasonable / reasonible** suggestion.

e) Chloe is a **terribly / terrably** good singer.

f) The class behaved very **sensibly / sensably** on their trip.

g) I will **possibly / possibley** be home by midday.

h) Oliver is a **dependable / dependible** friend.

i) That insect could be **identifible / identifiable** if we find a picture of it.

2 Add the correct **suffix**, -ible or -able, to the words in the boxes below.

| change_____ | comfort_____ | extend_____ |

| convert_____ | reason_____ | access_____ |

3 Add either <u>a</u> or <u>i</u> to complete the words in the sentences below. Write the full word correctly after each sentence.

a) You have acted very repons_bly. _____

b) The number four is divis_ble by two. _____

c) Some toys are very collect_ble. _____

d) This super hero was just about indescruct_ble. _____

e) We had an enjoy_ble day out. _____

/ 3

Total for this page

41

Suffixes: *-ant,-ance, -ancy, -ent, -ence, -ency*

To achieve 100 you need to correctly spell words with these suffixes.

1 Add the **suffix** -<u>ant</u> or -<u>ent</u> to the root below.

a) import_____

b) hesit_____

c) independ_____

d) intellig_____

e) assist_____

f) sil_____

g) brilli_____

h) confid_____

1
(1 mark)

2 Add two letters to complete each word.

a) Please can you help. This is an em___gency.

b) The dance perform___ce was exciting and new.

c) There is quite a di___ance between your house and mine.

d) You dog is highly obed___nt.

e) The storm was increasing in vi___ence each minute.

f) Add another number to this se___ence.

2
(1 mark)

3 Circle the correct **spelling** in each sentence.

a) Harry is **impatiant/impatient** to open his gift.

b) We should show **tolerance/tolerence** to one another.

c) The singer's **appearence/appearance** on stage was met with applause.

d) There will be a **consequance/consequence** to your actions.

3
(1 mark)

/3

Total for this page

Words with *ei*, *eigh*, *ey* and *ie/ei*

To achieve 100 you need to correctly spell words with these combinations of letters.

1 Add <u>ie</u> or <u>ei</u> to the words below.

a) Do you have many n__ighbours?

b) There are ___ght ducks on the pond.

c) The kittens have been up to misch__f.

d) Here is a p__ce of paper for you.

e) This bag w__ghs too much for me.

1
(1 mark)

2 Add one word from the box to complete each sentence below.

believe   ancient   receive   neither   prey

a) There is an _____ castle near my house.

b) I like _____ tea nor coffee.

c) Did you _____ my letter?

d) An eagle will _____ upon smaller birds.

e) Do you _____ in magic?

2
(1 mark)

3 Can you find a word in each cloud below? The first letter is given for you.

3
(1 mark)

sigleh   s_____

grein   r_____

tweigh   w_____

cedivee   d_____

zeesi   s_____

rieth   t_____

drifen   f_____

ifecre   f_____

/3
Total for this page

43

Words with *ough*

To achieve 100 you need to correctly spell words with this combination of letters.

1 Add a word from the box to each of the sentences below.

1
(1 mark)

brought   through   coughing   rough   ought

a) The sea is _____ today.

b) We need to go _____ the forest.

c) We have _____ some cake for you.

d) They _____ to take their coats as it may rain.

e) You have been _____ all day.

2 Circle the correct spelling.

2
(1 mark)

a) I **thought / thuoght** that Joe might win the race.

b) Jack gave his room a **through / thorough** clean.

c) The boxers **fought / fort** fairly.

d) Jay ate his dinner **allthough / although** he didn't enjoy it.

e) First make a **dough / douh** for your bread.

3 Use the letters in the cloud to make an <u>ough</u> word. The first letter is given for you.

3
(1 mark)

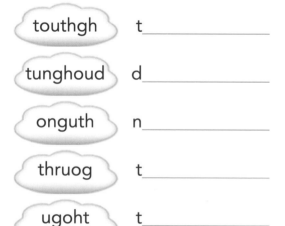

touthgh   t_____

tunghoud   d_____

onguth   n_____

thruog   t_____

ugoht   t_____

/3

Total for this page

44

Word endings: *al, el, il, le*

To achieve 100 you need to correctly spell words with these letters at the ends.

1 Circle the correct **spelling** for each sentence.

(1 mark)

a) The gymnast won a gold **medal / meddle**.

b) A **rumble / rumbel** of thunder could be heard.

c) A stone had to be removed from the child's **nostrul / nostril**.

d) Can you put these words in **alphabetical / alphabeticle** order?

e) Here is an **exampul / example** of what you need to do.

2 Add two letters to each of the words below to complete the spellings.

(1 mark)

a) Some food contains added chemic__ s.

b) If you swiv__ round on your chair, you will be able to see.

c) The cab__ s behind the computer are in a mess.

d) People in the desert still use cam__ s for transport.

e) It is tradition__ to give presents on birthdays.

3 Check the spelling of the el / al ending words in the passage below. Underline the **incorrect spellings** and write them correctly below.

(2 marks)

We were playing marbels in the garden but the gravle on the path kept making them tumble in the wrong directions. However, while so close to the ground, I saw a beautiful beetel with colours like jewles on its back. It was possibel to pick it up so I put it in a jar to show my teacher. She said it was not a regional example, but a tropicel one. What a discovery!

_____   _____   _____

_____   _____   _____

/ 4

Silent letters

To achieve 100 you need to correctly spell words with silent letters.

1 Add the correct **silent letter** to the words below.

   a) The _nuckle is a joint of your finger.

   b) Do you believe in g_osts?

   c) There are g_ards around the palace.

   d) Leaves fall from trees in the autum_.

   e) This is a lovely i_land.

   f) I have broken my _rist.

   g) The _nights supported the king.

   h) The si_n tells us to turn right.

   i) This field is full of this_les.

   j) Try to find the ans_er.

   1 (1 mark)

2 Underline all the words with **silent letters** in this passage.

   Mike told me that I was making the bread the wrong way. I had to knead the dough for ten minutes, but it was exhausting. I gave up because I knew I would not get the knack of it.

   2 (1 mark)

3 Add a word from the box to the sentences below.

honest writing doubt bomb column

   3 (1 mark)

   a) Put the largest numbers in the right _____ of your table.

   b) We have been _____ for hours.

   c) A good friend can be _____ with you even when it is hard to hear.

   d) I _____ that we will get there tonight.

   e) The soldiers managed to control the explosion of the _____.

/3

Total for this page

Homophones

To achieve 100 you need to correctly spell a variety of homophones.

1 Circle the correct **homophone** in each sentence.

a) I am **allowed/aloud** to go swimming.

b) Alfie has **passed/past** his driving test.

c) We **herd/heard** that you were ill.

d) I have left **your/you're** present on the table.

e) The sofa is **too/to** big for the doorway.

f) I think **you're/your** right.

g) The cyclist had to **break/brake** sharply to avoid an accident.

h) The children have put **there/their** books away.

i) Jim was looking for some **peace/piece** and quiet.

j) I never would have **guest/guessed** that it was you in disguise.

1 (1 mark)

2 Write a sentence to include each pair of **homophones**, or similar sounding words, below. Remember to punctuate your sentences correctly.

2 (7 marks)

groan   grown   _____

plane   plain   _____

isle   aisle   _____

desert   dessert   _____

our   hour   _____

sail   sale   _____

fought   fort   _____

3 Write <u>their</u>, <u>there</u> or <u>they're</u> to correctly complete each sentence below.

3 (1 mark)

a) It's so misty that I can't see over _____.

b) The twins made _____ best effort to be good.

c) I know _____ your sisters as you look so much alike.

!**Top tip**

- *They're* = They are
  Their = belonging to them
  There = indicates a place

/9

Total for this page

47

Synonyms and antonyms

To achieve 100 you need to know the terms synonym and antonym, and identify examples.

1 Which word is **closest** in meaning to <u>mishap</u>? Tick **one**.

argument ☐
accident ☐
prize ☐
reception ☐

1
(1 mark)

2 Which word is **opposite** in meaning to <u>abrupt</u>? Tick **one**.

never ☐
frequent ☐
slow ☐
sudden ☐

2
(1 mark)

3 Which word is the **antonym** of <u>surrender</u>? Tick **one**.

triumph ☐
fail ☐
improve ☐
deny ☐

3
(1 mark)

4 Which word is a **synonym** of <u>punctual</u>? Tick **one**.

burst ☐
late ☐
fast ☐
timely ☐

4
(1 mark)

5 Match the words below with their **antonyms**.

conscious	vanish
enough	confirm
appear	insufficient
deny	unaware

5
(1 mark)

> **! Top tips**
> - Remember:
>   S for synonym, S for same.
>   A for antonym, A for against (opposite to).
> - Double-check the question to know whether you are looking for similar or opposite meanings.

48

/ 5

Total for this page

Word families

To achieve 100 you need to know words that share the same root word or prefix.

1 Tick two words that belong to the same **word family**.

family ☐

famous ☐

familiar ☐

famine ☐

1
(1 mark)

2 Write the **root word** for this word family.

unworthy

worthwhile

_____

2
(1 mark)

3 Add another word to this **word family**.

activity

act

_____

3
(1 mark)

4 Tick **all** the words that belong to the same **word family**.

attention ☐

attendant ☐

inattentive ☐

unattractive ☐

4
(1 mark)

5 Add another word to this **word family**.

hard

_____

5
(1 mark)

/5

Total for
this page